Dressmaking

for Beginners

A Beginner's Guide to the Basics of Dressmaking so That You Can Use the Right Techniques and Methods to Quickly Sew the Dress Which Fits You Perfectly

By Nora Amlani

© **Copyright 2019 - All rights reserved.**

The content contained within this book may not be reproduced, duplicated or transmitted without direct written permission from the author or the publisher.

Under no circumstances will any blame or legal responsibility be held against the publisher or author for any damages, reparation, or monetary loss due to the information contained within this book. Either directly or indirectly.

Legal Notice:

This book is copyright protected. This book is only for personal use. You cannot amend, distribute, sell, use, quote or paraphrase any part, or the content within this book, without the consent of the author or publisher.

Disclaimer Notice:

Please note the information contained within this document is for educational and entertainment purposes only. All effort has been executed to present accurate, up to date and reliable, complete information. No warranties of any kind are declared or implied. Readers acknowledge that the author is not engaging in the rendering of legal, financial, medical or professional advice. The content within this book has been derived from various sources. Please consult a licensed professional before attempting any techniques outlined in this book.

By reading this document, the reader agrees that under no

circumstances is the author responsible for any losses, direct or indirect, which are incurred as a result of the use of information contained within this document, including, but not limited to, —errors, omissions, or inaccuracies.

Contents

Chapter 1-- Introduction 1

Chapter 2-- Figure 3

Chapter 3-- Selecting a Pattern Based Upon a Figure 9

    Flat Chest 9

    Big Bust 9

    Short Neck 10

    Thin Neck and Shoulders 10

    Short Full Figures 11

    Thin Tall Figures 11

    Big Hips 11

    Thick Waist 12

    Thick or Thin Upper Arms 12

Chapter 4-- Choosing the Fabric Color 13

    Redheads 14

    Blondes 14

    Brunettes 15

    White and Gray Haired Individuals 15

Chapter 5-- Style Lines, Balance, Silhouettes and Proportion 17

Chapter 6-- Fabric Choice-- Texture, Design, and Material 20

Chapter 7--Fibers and Fabrics 23

    Fabric Checklist 25

    Fabrics by Skill Level and User-Friendliness 27

    Beginners 27

    Semi-skilled 29

Skilled 36
Chapter 8-- Fabric Construction and Finishes............................... 39
Chapter 9-- How to Create Patterns 47
Chapter 10-- Dress Making Lingo... 50
Chapter 11--Label, Thread and Stitches... 54
Chapter 12-- Conclusion.. 57

Thank you for buying this book and I hope that you will find it useful. If you will want to share your thoughts on this book, you can do so by leaving a review on the Amazon page, it helps me out a lot.

Chapter 1-- Introduction

Fashion is a thing that is going to be constantly changing. Making your declaration or impact on the fashion business could be satisfying and lucrative in case you have the imagination to keep fashion brand-new and amazing. You could be a part of making a brand-new fashion trend by producing and designing your personal fashionably incredible dress.

In dressmaking, the greatest challenge to conquer is making a dress that is ideal for you. No 2 figures are precisely the same, so by creating your own clothes, you have the benefit over buying from the rack in understanding that the clothing you have on you was created only for you and your body. You attain the ideal fit that is most lovely for you.

Dressmaking is not as difficult as some people describe it. You could create a dress ideal for you by either studying currently created patterns and changing them to fit your body style, or you can produce your own dress by utilizing what you understand works for you. When you come up with a design, the rest is easy.

You could copy a currently prominent style on the marketplace, study fashion publications with the latest fads, or produce a scrapbook of numerous various styles of dresses you like and include various elements of each into a style of your own production. Nevertheless, you create your dress design; creating it yourself is going to be the most satisfying thing you do when it pertains to your fashion closet.

Chapter 2-- Figure

Since everybody's figure differs, you need to understand your figure and all of its drawbacks. This is going to make it simpler for you to pick a lovely dress style for you, whether it is by a currently made pattern or a pattern you design by yourself.

Picking a pattern could be enjoyable, particularly if you have currently done your research and understand what's in and what is going to always be in, like the little black dress. You can discover a wide range of dress patterns on the web or at your neighborhood fabric shop. When you have the design of the dress in mind, pattern books can provide an intriguing quantity of variations of the specific fundamental design.

The skirt part might interest you more on a certain pattern then the other, and the bodice might attract you more, or neckline, or sleeve style, and so on. You coul take these various elements of a dress, combine them into one, and produce your own pattern/design. When taking a look at a range of patterns, have a pencil and a bit of paper nearby to write down ideas and pattern numbers to make it simpler for you when you are prepared to devote yourself. Frequently, out of date pattern books could be found at fabric shops for a really small price if not free. This is an excellent way to begin a library of various ideas.

Patterns have plenty of different figure types. Figure types are organized based upon proportion and height and based on 2 primary measurements-- height, and waist to neck length. Pick your pattern(s) to fit your figure type. To discover your figure type stand before a mirror in only your underwear that would generally be worn beneath your dress. Measure your of bust, hips and waist. Get somebody to assist you in taking your measurements of height and waist to neck length. Waist to neck length ought to be drawn from your backside for the greatest fitting bodice. Contrast these measurements with that of a size chart. For instance, in case your bust measured 35 inches, hips 37 inches and waist 26 inches, you would be looking at a dress size of lady's 14. Select your pattern sizes appropriately. When your measurements fall in between 2 classified sizes, constantly pick the bigger size of the two. That leaves you space for making changes to make your garment suit you completely.

In the following part, you are going to discover a Measurement Keeper. Create one for anybody you plan on sewing for.

Here are certain fundamental rules to utilize when obtaining these measurements. Constantly have a second set of hands to attain the ideal measurements. In case you are still uncertain about taking measurements, you could constantly have it expertly performed for you.

Height: Stand on the ground, barefoot, with your back versus the wall. Look straight in front of you. On the wall, Chalk a small line at the level of the top of the head. Measure from the ground to this line.

Bust: Measure at the most full bust portion.

Waist: connect a string piece around your waist. Measure the string, but do not get rid of it. Keep the string there for additional measurements.

Hips: Put the tape around the fullest figure area. This is normally around 9 inches beneath the waist for misses and ladies, and 7 inches beneath the waist for miss petite, junior petite, half size, and young teen/ junior.

Back-- neck to waist: Locate the bone that stands out at the neck nape and measure from here down to the center of the midsection.

Shoulder width: Clasp your hands together ahead of the midsection. With arms somewhat raised and forward, measure along the back from shoulder to shoulder.

Back width-- armhole to armhole: Measure along the back at the level of the shoulder blade. Begin and wrap up where the regular armhole seams are.

Shoulder length-- right and left: Measure from the neck base to the shoulder point on every side. These measurements might be somewhat different.

Front bodice-- center front, left and right: (Center) Measure from the neckline directly down to the midsection. (Left and right) Measure from the shoulder seam placement to the midsection on every side, across the bust.

Side bodice-- left and right: Stand with hands on hips and measure every side from an inch beneath the underarm down to the midsection. There might be a minor distinction on every side in measurement.

Chest-- on bust at the front and atop the bust: (Above) Measure around at the level of the underarm over the bust. (Bust ahead) Measure from underarm seam to underarm seam across the bust. In case the measurement is 2 inches or more than the width of the back, your pattern might need to be changed to enable more space.

Chest-- diaphragm: Do this measurement around the rib cage, halfway in between the fullest bust area and the waist.

Shoulder to elbow: Flex your arm and take measurement from the shoulder point to the elbow point.

Sleeve length: Flex the arm a little and take measurement from the the wrist to the shoulder point, involving the flex. It is additionally useful to measure 1 inch from beneath the seam of the underarm to the wrist with the arm directly.

Wrist: Take the measurement of the wrist over the wrist bone.

Neck to hem: Take the measurement from the neck nape to the needed hem level of dress. Have the tape at the waist while you measure.

Waist to hem: Holding measuring tape at the waist, measure to the needed hem level.

Chapter 3-- Selecting a Pattern Based Upon a Figure

As specified previously, no 2 figures are precisely the same. One might fit the basic measurement chart completely, whereas another might just compare in a couple of areas. An individual could be flat-chested, and in the bust department be a size 7 yet in the hips and waist fall in size 14. The following is going to aid you in identifying what looks ideal on differing figure types.

Flat Chest

Flat chested ladies fair much better with draped and gathered styles, so the bodice has actually included fullness that is more lovely. Flat chested ladies ought to stay away from broad necklines or fitted bodice.

Big Bust

Big busted ladies ought to stay away from high necklines, drapes, heavy frills, and gathered bodices. Full sleeves additionally ought to be stayed away from, as they are going to make a lady seem top-heavy, throwing off a lovely appearance. Big busted ladies are going to fair much better with a tailored top bodice with fitted sleeves. Leave any trims for the skirt area, unless heavy hipped.

Short Neck

Stay away from tie neckbands, turtlenecks, mandarin necklines, broad shoulder lines and high polo necks. Plunging long necklines are much more lovely if you have a short neck in addition to neckline in a V-shape with narrow shoulder lines like in tank style.

Thin Neck and Shoulders

In case you have narrow shoulders and a slim neck, it is ideal to stay away from dress patterns which sport a boat or broad style neckline. You are going to be more impressed by necklines in V-shape, mandarin standing collar or tie collars.

Short Full Figures

Short full-figured ladies are impressed more by dress styles with gored skirts, fitted sleeves, and/or princess lines. Stay away from broad full sleeves, necks, frills, gathered skirts, horizontal stripes and broad belts.

Thin Tall Figures

Ladies of slim figures and height are impressed by draped or gathered skirts accentuated with neck trim and broad belts. Stay away from fitted bodices, straight skirts and princess lines.

Big Hips

Stay away from pockets at hips, fitted skirts and narrow bodices. Search for patterns with shaped skirts from the waist which are gathered just when the waist is little.

Thick Waist

Stay away from broad belts, cummerbunds, and slim skirts. Tapered lines, narrow belts, and gored skirts are going to impress you more.

Thick or Thin Upper Arms

Both thick and thin upper arms ought to stay away from sleeveless style dress bodice. Rather, choose 3/4 length sleeves or cap sleeves.

Chapter 4-- Choosing the Fabric Color

By donning a color which is not lovely to you could alter the way your body figure presents in addition to making your complexion appear dull? Selecting the appropriate dress color is just as crucial as the figure style. In case the color isn't for you, regardless of how good the dress is created, the impact is going to be completely lost.

There are a couple of things one needs to understand when picking the appropriate garment color. The old-time misconceptions of donning greens and blues, and pinks and reds together are no longer accurate. Basically, nowadays, everything goes, if it complements you! Blending and matching colors that match you could be enjoyable and provide your production your very own private touch. Year to year, what is taken into consideration as "in fashion" when it comes to color changes. Do not provide the season color as much importance as what looks excellent on you! Picking the appropriate colors could shift attention far from figure faults you might have. Accentuating your dress with accessories in contrasting or matching colors could even highlight your design additionally.

Colors could produce an optical illusion. For example, cool dark colors make you look tinier, while warm light colors make you look bigger. Subtle muted colors could be slendering, and brilliant contrasting colors can accentuate one's figure, making it look bigger. Here are certain basic guidelines to assist in guiding you in what is going to look most lovely to you. Nevertheless, they are simply basic guidelines, and some exceptions could apply.

Redheads

The basic guideline for redheads is to stay away from colors which match the color tone of their hair, color, and stay away from reds, oranges and pinks. Select natural colors like grays, camel, cream, black, browns, and white for the primary color. Accents or contrast trims in yellows, blues and greens complement redheads well.

Blondes

Stay away from some oranges and yellows. Blondes look awesome in pastel blues, browns and greens.

For mousy blonde-haired people and dark blonde-haired individuals, opt for rich deep colors.

Brunettes

Brown-haired ladies are most likely the most fortunate of all hair colors when it pertains to color shades that appear fantastic on them. They can quickly pull off nearly any bright-colored fabric, browns, blacks, and whites.

White and Gray Haired Individuals

Pastel shades are excellent for these hair shades, nevertheless, shallow skin requires warm colors without excessive yellow to provide it an enticing tone. Pale skin requires colors that are sufficiently strong to create contrast, and dark skin is just like brunettes. Dark-skinned individuals could pull off almost any color, even though exotic colors throughout the day could seem out of place on them.

There are 3 kinds of clothing color schemes, and those are contrasting, monochrome, and toning. Constantly have a go at color schemes by holding the fabric mix close to your face as you are looking in a mirror to see if the colors fit you. Monochrome color schemes utilize shades of one color or one color with white and black. Contrasting color schemes utilize 2 or more various colors in differing strengths that match one another. Toning color schemes utilize 2 or more comparable colors.

Chapter 5-- Style Lines, Balance, Silhouettes and Proportion

Style lines of a dress coul highlight or hide figure parts. It is necessary that if there is anything that is not pleasing to you when it comes to your figure, that you pick the ideal style line for your dress pattern that is going to assist to downplay that fault. There are 3 various kinds of style lines--Horizontal, Vertical and Curved. Each specific style line accentuates a body in a different way. Vertical style lines include height and make a figure appearance thinner. The princess style is an instance of a vertical style line. Horizontal lines have a tendency to include a width appearance.

These ought to just be utilized to flatter various points of one's figure. Curved seams produce soft and lovely lines. Curved style lines are additionally frequently described as draping. Diagonal lines go from left to right when seeing a garment, and lengthy diagonal lines take the eye down in a slendering line. Utilize care when utilizing lines that show up in the pattern or weave. Straight lines are normally extreme and provide a tailored or traditional appearance where drapes and curves appear stylish and womanly.

The standard dress garment shapes could be broken down into 4 classifications-- semi-fitted, fitted, somewhat fitted, and loosely fitted. Fitted dress garments fit the bodies natural curves and might flaunt your figure. Fitted dress garments need to be properly cut and thoroughly fitted. Caution: This style might crease easily. Semi-fitted dress garments are typically fitted in the bust location with a somewhat looser cut at the hips and waist. This style is more lovely for the less than ideal figure.

Somewhat fitted dress garments are simple to use and permit space for motion. They simply barely follow the outline of the body and might be bias cut. The loosely fitted dress garment is typically fitted just on the shoulders, with the remainder presenting full.

Any garment appears greatest when details are not in simply one place. Preserve balance by keeping an equivalent quantity of eye appeal in 2 or more garment areas. 2 halves might be same, so the dress has a balanced appearance. In case one place has a special focus, it might be balanced with another point of interest somewhere else. Proportion is essential when relating dress parts to your figure and one another. Take into account style lines, fabric, design details, figure type and pattern. The size and scale of the dress and fabric need to additionally fit the figure type.

A full mid-skirt style dress might swamp a small thin figure while a mini-skirt style dress is uncomplimentary on a high, plump figure. Pleasing proportions could be attained by organizing the dress in quarters, thirds and halves. For certain figures, somewhat irregular proportions might be preferable. It is the total appearance that is essential. To get an idea of how your dress is going to appear on you when finished, go to dress shops and try out the dress that resembles the style you want to create. Hold various fabrics up to you and see what appears ideal.

Check the impact of glossy versus dull fabrics, small and big prints, sheer in contrast to large fabrics, and different color mixes prior to selecting what kind of fabric you wish to utilize in your design.

Chapter 6-- Fabric Choice-- Texture, Design, and Material

Your fabric texture is going to impact the last appearance of a garment. The fabric could be flowing or stiff, smooth or rough, dull or shiny, and sheer or large. Clingy, soft fabrics expose the figure while stiff fabric might hide a figure's fault by producing a smooth outline. Large or shiny materials make the figure seem bigger. Those kinds of fabrics are much better utilized for those who might be too thin. Somebody who is heavy ought to stay away from large or glossy fabrics unless they are utilized as accessories or trim. Soft clinging fabrics like jersey, wool, crepes, bias-cut silk, and make for good soft womanly dresses.

Soft loosely woven fabrics like heavy wool, jerseys and crepes make attractive flared clothes or dresses with un-pressed pleats. Gently woven fabrics could be draped nearer to the body. Strongly woven wool, cotton, linen, fine tweed and silk make customized clothes with a sculptured or seamed appearance.

Patterns and prints can include appeal and interest to a dress. Think about the function and style of the dress when utilizing a print. A lot of seams and other style details might separate the fabric print, making it tough not to discover seams. It could additionally be tough to match the pattern of the print, providing your dress an incomplete or off look. The more complex the design of the print is, the more difficult it is to have the pattern in unison.

When utilizing a print or pattern, pick suited to your figure in color and size. Little patterns are prettier on small figures, while bigger patterns might be frustrating. Vertical stripes make a figure appear taller and slimmer while horizontal stripes include width and decrease height appearance. sharp contrast and intense colors make a figure additionally seem bigger.

The primary color ought to be lovely. Utilize mixes of other colors in little places like in printed pockets on a plain dress. Limit distinctive designs to places where they are complementary and do not accentuate figure faults. The angles and curves of dress designs and fabric ought to be in harmony. Straight blocky bodices appear much better in checks than paisleys. Curved bodice collars and seams might ruin a striped or plaid impact. Additionally, take into account the pattern direction and what you plan on being the natural dress flow, so they don't conflict.

When creating your dress, you are going to wish to make certain you buy enough material plus some more just in case of a misstep. Measure the length from the neck nape to the wanted hemline. Double this measurement and include 5 1/4 inches for hem and seam allowance. Brief sleeves are going to require an extra 18 inches and long sleeves 27 inches. A complete skirt requires one additional waist to hem length.

Chapter 7--Fibers and Fabrics

There is absolutely nothing worse than purchasing fabric yards for a dress you have actually imagined in your head to get it home, spread it out, and recognize that it is simply not suited for the garment. The information to follow is going to assist you in choosing a fabric appropriate for that unique dress distinct to only you.

The majority of pattern envelopes provide an idea regarding which fabrics go ideally with that specific pattern. That does not imply that those are the only fabrics that could be utilized, however, it does offer you a basic idea regarding what kind of weave and texture of the fabric is preferable. The fabric picked ought to fit the individual for who the dress is meant for; if you are creating it for yourself, then it ought to flatter your skin tone, hair color, and be of such material to hide figure imperfections in addition to working with planned pattern and design of the dress. A heavy, large fabric would not work that good with a dress pattern meant to have more motion unless you are deliberately attempting to get rid of the motion aspect.

High slim figures must not put on vertical stripes. If the natural skin tone is extremely colored, do not put on multicolor prints. Big designs, shiny fabrics or horizontal stripes do not complement plump, short figures.

Do not select a fabric that has a busy design when creating a dress with pin tucking, uncommon lines, or other stitching detail. The design is going to sidetrack from the completed impact, and the numerous hours of handwork you invest into your design might go undetected.

The fabric ought to be a proper knit or weave for the dress style you are creating. For tight fitting garments, select carefully woven fabrics, and for loose-fitting dresses, select loosely woven fabrics. Ensure the fabrics you select are quickly cleaned or washable, depending upon the quantity of wear your dress is going to get. In case you are creating a sundress that is going to be worn more frequently, utilize a fabric which is washable by a machine. If you are creating a special event dress, then, certainly, take into consideration a few of the fantastic dry clean only fabrics or those that require additional care.

When picking fabrics to be worn together, stay away from the muddled effect. If you wish to blend fabrics, have at least one common aspect, like design or color. A range of plain fabrics might be utilized together. Any patterned fabric which highlights one plain color could be added.

Do not overlook texture. Compare fabrics and attempt to have a contrast in texture. If it is tough to select color schemes with balanced color and design, copy concepts from books or magazines and check out your notes taken when you tried out various dresses when searching for styles that matched your figure.

Fabric Checklist

Ask yourself these questions when choosing a fabric best fit for your pattern.

1. Is it stiff or soft?
2. Is it going to drape?
3. Is it going to extend and recover its shape?
4. Is it going to shrink?
5. Is it washable, or does it have to be dry cleaned?
6. Is it clingy?
7. Is it scratchy or rough?
8. Is it stain and soil-resistant?
9. Is it going to be warm or cool?
10. Is it absorbent?

11. Is it colorfast?
12. How does it handle?
13. Is it going to require ironing?

Utilize common sense. E.g., If you don't require a fabric which drapes, then when asking yourself question 2. If the response is yes, then you would not buy that fabric. Your fabric will make or break your dress. You wish to ensure not just that the fabric you pick is simple to deal with if you are a beginner to sewing, but that it matches your design as well. Here are several other basic rules for examining the fabric you are creating for your dress.

Inspect the fabric over properly for any flaws. Flaws are frequent in lots of fabrics. Nevertheless, if there are a lot, it is going to make it hard, if not inconceivable, for you to be able to work around them. Inspect the fabric grain to make certain it is straight. If not, could you make it straight with a bit of effort? If not, select some other fabric. Constantly encertain there is enough of the wanted fabric you desire on one bolt. Buying the fabric from different bolts could be devastating.

Even though they might appear identical, the dye lot might be off in one of the bolts, which is going to throw off your completed garment. Examine the orientation of your fabric too. Encertain it has the wrong and right side if it ought to hold true. Certain fabrics are reversible; nevertheless, they still have a prominent side. Try to find and comprehend the pattern direction, if there is one.

Fabrics by Skill Level and User-Friendliness

Pick patterns based upon your own private sewing capability level. If you are a novice, stay away from patterns in the couturier area. Start with simple to stitch patterns and work your way up as your capability levels establish.

Beginners

Cotton: Strong and quickly washed fabric created from natural fiber from cotton linters. This fabric is comfy and ranges from smooth, fine, thick toweling to voile.

- Benefits: Easy to push and deal with. Gathers properly and could be tucked. It could be embroidered and is frequently reversible.

- Drawbacks: None

Gingham: Plain-woven fabric. Normally, dyed yarn threads create a visible check pattern on a white background.

- Benefits: Easy to push and deal with, gathers effectively, patterned on each side.

- Drawbacks: Does not pleat effectively.

Yard: Light woven cloth utilized in bodices of dresses as well as handkerchiefs and blouses.

- Benefits: Does not fray. Crisp yet simple to deal with. Easy to push and gathers effectively.

- Drawbacks: Doesn't have any

Pique: Securely woven fabric w/ horizontal ribs.

- Benefits: Does not fray. Maintains shape and wears effectively.

- Drawbacks: Too springy for gathering. Needs matching ribs.

Poplin: Plain-woven fabric with fine horizontal ribs.

- Benefits: Does not fray. Solid to deal with, gathers properly and effortlessly pushed.

- Drawbacks: Doesn't have any

Seersucker: Woven fabric with noticeable, general surface design.

- Benefits: Does not fray. Easy to deal with, light pushing required, gathers, and hangs effectively.

- Drawbacks: Could not be pleated or tucked. If patterned, matching seams could be hard.

Semi-skilled

Wool Boucle: Medium weight wool with looped piling.

- Benefits: Does not crease, is light-weight and drapes and hangs effectively.

- Drawbacks: Stitching could be hard to keep straight in case the weave is heavy. Will not pleat easily.

<u>Chintz</u>: Plain-woven, solid-colored or printed, glazed cotton fabric.

- Benefits: Does not fray. Easy to push. Hangs effectively.

- Drawbacks: Could not be gathered in case of too high glaze. Tough to manage.

<u>Cotton Satin</u>

- Benefits: Does not fray. Strong, hangs and presses effectively, frequently crease-resistant, and gathers and tucks well.

- Drawbacks: Doesn't have any

<u>Crepe</u>: Light to medium fabric with a textured appearance.

- Benefits: Tucks, gathers, drapes and hangs effectively. It could be embroidered.

- Drawbacks: Springy

<u>Crepe De Chine</u>: Luxurious shiny light-weight fabric with a subtle texture.

- Benefits: Does not fray terribly. Easy to manage and typically reversible.

- Drawbacks: Ironed boosts could be difficult to get rid of.

<u>Denim</u>: Strong twill weaved fabric typically created from cotton. It is washable and available in every color, yet typically, it is blue.

- Benefits: Does not fray terribly. Long-wearing, pleats effectively and is powerful.

- Drawbacks: Does not gather quickly. Shrinks when cleaned.

Wool Flannel

- Benefits: Does not fray. Pleats and hangs effectively. Helpful for tailored, styled dresses.

- Drawbacks: Doesn't have any

Wool Gabardine

- Benefits: Great for tailored designs, pleats effectively and is powerful.

- Drawbacks: Doesn't have any

Linen: Natural made material from the ripe flax plant stalks. Linen is a long-wearing and sturdy fabric.

- Benefits: Pleats, drapes, hangs, and presses effectively. Ideal for tailored clothes and maintains its shape well.

- Drawbacks: Creases and tears terribly.

Muslin: Plain-woven cotton fabric created in numerous weights.

- Benefits: Good for fine sewing. It could be frilled and tucked.

- Drawbacks: Frays; and shrinks when cleaned.

Organdy: Plain-woven light fabric that has a crisp finish.

- Benefits: Perfect for stitching. It could be rolled, tucked and helpful for hand or sewing machine embroidery.

- Drawbacks: Springy, does not gather effectively, frays to some degree, and is transparent. Shrinks after being washed.

Sateen: Sturdy cotton fabric built in a satin weave with a shiny face

- Benefits: Other materials could be utilized over it without it clinging.

- Drawbacks: Frays. It could slip while being sliced or stitched.

Lingerie Satin

- Benefits: Could be gathered, tucked and embroidered. Drapes and hangs effectively,

- Drawbacks: Frays quickly.

Wool Serge: resilient twill weave fabric, weighs more than gabardine, created from a mix of 55% polyester and 45% wool.

- Benefits: Holds pleats and does not crease quickly.

- Drawbacks: Doesn't have any

Silk: Naturally created fabric from the silkworm. Silk is a warm, sturdy, absorbent and springy fabric.

- Benefits: Gathers and pleats quickly. Sturdy yet soft. Suitable for fine sewing. Maintains shape, drapes and hangs effectively.

- Drawbacks: Frays terribly.

<u>Polyester Wool</u>

- Benefits: Does not crease quickly. and holds pleats.

- Drawbacks: Frays quickly. It could be large to put on.

<u>Voile</u>: Light plain-woven fabric with an open weave typically utilized for bodices of dresses, shirts and blouses.

- Benefits: Great for fine sewing. It could be frilled or tucked.

- Drawbacks: Frays quickly. Seams need to be sturdy and strengthened.

<u>Worsted Wool</u>

- Benefits: Pleats effectively, durable material, and ideal for each tailored style dress.

- Drawbacks: Hard to work on. It tends to be large and extremely combustible unless dealt with.

Skilled

Chiffon: Soft light-weight plain-woven fabric.

- Benefits: Drapes, hangs and gathers effectively.

- Drawbacks: Frays quickly. Needs competent handling.

Georgette: Durable, large, light-weight silk with a crinkly, matte surface.

- Benefits: Drapes, hangs and gathers effectively. Does not fray quickly.

- Drawbacks: Edges and seams might extend.

Jersey

- Benefits: Hangs and drapes effectively.

- Drawbacks: Edges have a tendency to extend. Deal with it carefully, so the material is not misshaped. Stitch with a stretch stitch.

Moiré

- Benefits: Gathers, hangs and flares effectively while preserving crispness.

- Drawbacks: Frays terribly. It reveals watermarks and could be challenging to match patterns at seams.

<u>Nylon</u>: Nylon is created from items of the oil industry. It is typically mixed with cotton or wool. Utilized by itself, nylon brings in dirt due to static electrical power.

- Benefits: It does not need much pushing. It is fine yet durable.

- Drawbacks: Frays quickly and it is transparent.

<u>Taffeta</u>: Plain-- woven fabric that has a crisp feel, frequently utilized to line garments.

- Benefits: Could be elegant.

- Drawbacks: Frays terribly.

<u>Velour</u>: Fabric with a cut stack surface. Typically created from cotton or silk, however, is now available in man-made fibers. It is crease-resistant and washable; nevertheless, the pile on velvet might be squashed if not dealt with thoroughly.

- Benefits: Drapes and hangs effectively.

- Drawbacks: Can just be sliced in one direction. Tough to press. Pins are going to mark the stack, so utilize just really fine needles.

Chapter 8-- Fabric Construction and Finishes

From man-made to natural yarn fibers, stunning fabrics are being created. The most typical manners in which yarn is formed into the fabric are knitting and weaving, and a couple less typical methods of felting and bonding. As soon as the fabric has been built, there are lots of finishes which have actually been created to enhance the performance or appearance of fabrics. The finishes are constantly administered to the finished fabric, not the specific yarn threads utilized in the construction.

Let's take a look at the manner in which fabric is built initially. The procedure by which fabric is built identifies how the fabric responds. If it has any stretch whatsoever, if it is large, and how powerful it is, all things essential to understand when selecting the appropriate fabric.

Weaving is the procedure where 2 yarn groups are combined at appropriate angles in woven fabric. Warp is the thread which goes parallel to the selvage. Warp threads are the toughest of the weave. In the weave, the crosswise thread (weft) goes beneath and above the warp threads, producing the weave, which produces the fabric. The more weave threads there are, the more powerful the fabric. There are numerous weave variations-- basket, rib, twill, pile, satin, jacquard and dobby. You could notice these variations if you take a look at your fabric using a magnifying glass.

Knitting is a continual yarn which is knitted into interlocking loops to create an elastic, versatile fabric. This could be performed by knitting machines or by hand. Manufacturers are able to knit on knitting machines, a substantial range of textures and weights of knit fabrics. A couple of terms utilized in knitting fabric are:

- Wale: The loop row going lengthwise within the warp threads.

- Course: The crosswise rows.

- Denier: Term utilized for the density and weight of the knit fabric.

- Gage: The amount of stitches utilized to form a particular fabric row. The greater the gage, the tighter the knit.

The yarn could be weft-knitted into a tubular or flat fabric by utilizing a single continual thread which connects with the following and previous rows. When more then a single yarn is utilized to create lengthwise loop rows, it is referred to as a warp knit. Every loop row connects with the other ones on either side. Fabrics that are created by doing this are usually run proof.

Bonding is a less frequent method to create fabric. Fibers are bound together without weaving or knitting. There is no grain, and the bonded fabric is without stretch. These fabrics are not laminated or self-lined, which implies 2 materials are merged together. It would resemble taking single yarn strands, laying them alongside, and gluing them together to create one piece of material.

Felting is an affordable warm, non woven fabric. Fabrics manufacturers create felted material from fur or wool fibers amalgamated by heat, wetness, pressure and friction. Felt is created in numerous densities and colors. It does not fray, yet it normally is not resilient enough for many clothes. There is another type of felting which is performed by using knitted fabric. It is performed comparably to that of the production method, just on a much tinier scale. When wool yarns are knitted to create a fabric, by putting them within a hot bath, that is within a washing machine, the once knitted yarn fabric is going to come out looking like felt while also being very sturdy.

Numerous finishes have actually been created to enhance the functionality and look of the fabric. Without several finishes, particular materials would not be appropriate for clothing wear, like the flameproof finish you are going to read on the label of kids' sleepwear. Certain frequent finishes you are going to see on bulk fabric labels are:

- Colorfast: What this suggests is that when you clean your finished garment, it is not going to lose its color or bleed.

- Flameproof: This is administered to the fabric to make certain it is flame proof. The law demands that all kids' sleepwear is treated with a flameproof finish. Here is the issue though, even though they might be treated with a flameproof finish, frequently these finishes diminish during washing, so don't utilize the label too much as a convenience element.

- London-Shrunk: This is when wool suiting is moistened and left to naturally dry prior to tailoring.

- Luster: Starches and resins are administered to the cotton fabric to create a glossy and crisp surface, similar to chintz. (Note: This also disappears due to washings.).

- Machine Washable: A finish is administered to the fabric to render it washable. Along with the typical fabrics, it is feasible to wash certain leathers, suede's and wools in a washing machine in case they have actually been dealt with. Try to find the label for laundering directions when buying the fabric.

- Mercerizing: The procedure of treating cotton in tension to provide it with durability and render it shiny.

- Permanent Press: A procedure performed by the maker to stop fabrics from creasing and to maintain the shape without needing ironing.

- Preshrink: When a maker shrinks the material down to lower the quantity of shrinking during laundering.

- Waterproofing: When a maker utilizes silicone on the fabric surface to render it water repellant.

- Sizing or Dressing: Glue, wax or clay is included to a fabric to give it body. Nevertheless, it does ultimately wash out.

Many fabrics extend a bit. Some yarn mage fabrics are created with integrated stretch created by tight crimping or twisting yarn. Special expendable fibers might be utilized, or the fibers might include a fine rubber core which provides them its spring back quality. Knit fabrics created from these kinds of yarn have the most stretch or give. Fabrics utilized for sportswear stretch in each directions. Weft- stretch or warp- stretch just stretch in a single direction.

When picking and utilizing a stretch fabric, make certain the pattern you are utilizing is for that specific kind of fabric. Follow the pattern instructions thoroughly. Stretch material could be difficult to deal with for your initial number of times. While on the machine, you might tend to pull the fabric to taunt, which is going to leave buckles in your seams. Purchase the remnants of stretch fabric and practice with stretch fabric prior to cutting an entire dress pattern out and trying to stitch your dress. Even though you could rip out the seams and begin again, the majority of stretch fabrics are not really forgiving

Self-lined fabrics were, at one time, referred to as bonded fabrics. A few of the initial bonded fabrics provided garments a "stuck-out" look and they were stiff. Today's self-lined fabrics are created to be wearer friendly, drape perfectly, and are done for an added look. Self-lined fabric is simple to deal with on the machine and is an excellent starter fabric next to cotton. Self-lined fabrics could save you money and time. Rather than cutting the fabric for the dress and a lining fabric, you just need to cut one fabric and stitch one fabric! Plus, you are obtaining 2 fabrics for the cost of one!

The fabric withstands fraying, which decreases the requirement for finishing edges, which is extremely lengthy. The included lining makes it a lot easier to create buttonholes as well. The lining helps it move on the sewing machine, minimizing the dangers of twisting checks or patterns out of shape. Garments created with self-lined fabrics maintain their shape and maintain a tailored appearance a lot longer than other fabric kinds. They do not bag nor crease.

Chapter 9-- How to Create Patterns

After you have actually been stitching for some time, you might have gathered several patterns along the way. Ensure that when you buy a pattern to take excellent care of it since once you have actually been stitching for some time, you might wish to try creating your own patterns.

There might be particular elements you like from various patterns, like a collar on one, the sleeves on another, the skirt, or the bodice on another. By conserving all your patterns, you can start to blend and match these wanted elements to produce your own original design. You could create copies of your initial patterns on pelon, fabric like muslin, or on an unprinted newspaper which you can receive from any newspaper publisher in bulk. Many times, they have end rolls which they are not able to utilize. These are excellent for copying your patterns and lengthening their duration, inexpensively.

Any sewer can gain from utilizing a mock-up pattern referred to as a fitting shell, basic pattern, or toile. A standard paper pattern is thoroughly adapted to your private measurements. It is sliced and tacked together in a fabric like muslin. The mock garment is fitted thoroughly and precisely to your figure. After having this mock pattern built, all your brand-new patterns could be contrasted to it prior to sewing and cutting to prevent errors. It might take longer to examine the fit of every pattern by doing this, however, it could be worthwhile, particularly when details truly matter. In this manner, you can always do a trial run on muslin prior to dedicating yourself to the real fabric you wish your dress to be created from.

You could absolutely mix 2 or more patterns to build your own distinct dress. Nevertheless, it is ideal if they are all in the identical size range unless you are really proficient in pattern modifications. If unsure, do it in muslin initially.

The issue with commercially created patterns is they are created for a nonspecific individual, not for your special figure. You might need to make numerous pattern changes to create a commercial pattern fit appropriately. Another way you can form your own patterns is by garments you currently own that you understand fit you well. You can thoroughly take apart the garment and trace it onto newsprint, including 1/2 inch for seam allowance.

If you do not wish to take apart a presently owned garment, another choice is to hit your neighborhood thrift shops and locate garments that suit you well, no matter the color or print. These are not going to matter. This is an inexpensive way to get garments that could be created into patterns for a custom dress pattern.

Chapter 10-- Dress Making Lingo

There is a lot of lingo you are going to encounter when stitching, be it a shirt, skirt, a dress, or a set of slacks. If you do not know the terms, it would resemble following instructions in a language you do not understand.

Some popular terms utilized relating to fabrics are grain-line, selvage, nap and bias. Selvage is the finished woven material edge. In some cases, the producer's name and style of the fabric might be printed along this edge. The function of a selvage edge is to stop the material from unraveling or fraying. The grain-line (in some cases described as the straight line) of fabric are the threads going parallel to the selvage. The crosswise grain are the threads which go from selvage to selvage.

You ought to constantly attempt to cut with the grain-line when feasible. Bias describes the thread line which is diagonal to the crosswise grain and grain-line. In case a fabric is pulled along the bias, it is going to extend. A garment is going to hang in a different way based upon the direction it has been sliced. The fabric nap describes the manner in which the stack lays. It is a soft raised surface frequently discovered on wool fabrics.

Similar to fur, when you run your hand on it a certain way it feels smooth, while the incorrect way of nap is going to feel rough. When creating a dress, you wish to make certain the nap runs all in the identical direction. The nap is one method to differentiate which fabric side is the front or face.

Certain additional terms you might discover are:

- A-line: A skirt or dress which looks like an overview of an "A."

- Avant-Garde: Beyond the trend.

- Bateau: Neckline following the collar bone curve.

- Caftan: Long streaming coatlike dress often with bell sleeves.

- Coat-Dress: Front opening dress that has the coat look.

- Couture: Garment created all manually.

- Décolleté: Shoulders and neck, and a plunging neckline.

- Mandarin: Narrow standing collar, close-fitting at the neck.

- Maxi: Length of the hem in between ankle and mid-calf.

- Micro: Length of the hem going to upper thigh.

- Midi: Length of the hem going to mid-calf.

- Mini: Length of the hem falling at mid-thigh.

- Peplum: Little flounce around the garment hips, generally as an bodice extension.

- Princess line: Garment suited with seams rather than darts.

- Sheath: Close-fitting dress which has a straight skirt.

- Shift: Casual loose fitting dress.

- Skirt-waist: Dress and a bodice buttoned as a t-shirt.

- Toile: Copy of an initial design of the garment created in cotton fabric, like muslin.

- Tunic: Straightforward dress worn over a garment.

- Voile: Plain-woven, light fabric which has an open weave, typically utilized in dresses, skirts and blouses.

Chapter 11--Label, Thread and Stitches

When you create a garment, regardless of if it is a dress, you ought to constantly place an information label on it. Unless you have them jotted down, you might forget essential care information for the fabric utilized. Even if it is simply a handwritten tag connected to the hanger you put your end product on, ensure it is there. In case you own a sewing machine that permits monogramming, you could develop your own designer labels. There is additionally iron on fabric and monogramming care labels which you could buy from a fabric provider. The label ought to consist of fiber content, special finishes, trim information, fabric construction, ironing directions, and any other important data.

The fundamental sewing machine has 3 stitch settings kinds, regular, zigzag and blasting. There might be a number of various settings for these stitches. Those variations establish how many stitches are going to be placed within an inch. The regular stitch is utilized for the majority of straight seams, with many utilizing 10 to 12 stitches per inch. The basting stitch is a lengthier stitch with less stitches per inch and is utilized to hold a seam together momentarily while you are dealing with other things. A basting stitch is really simple to get rid of, and because there are only a couple of stitches per inch, the majority of fabrics are going to tolerate it. Nevertheless, you could hand stitch tacking or basting stitches by hand too. The zigzag stitch is utilized for décor or to finish raw edges.

If you plan on hand sewing, there are a number of hand stitches which could include so much more character to your garment then you might ever accomplish by machine. Nevertheless, nowadays, there are sewing machines which could do nearly anything except cutting out the pattern. Some are now computer accentuated carrying out lots of hand stitches that were, at one time, never ever possible to carry out automotive. For those who still delight in the standard ways of sewing, there are lots of fantastic books that are loaded with the most lovely hand stitches referred to as the French knots, arrowhead tack, featherstitch, lazy daisy stitch, chain stitch, and a lot more.

There is a wide variety of sewing thread, each has its special function, and it is essential to utilize the appropriate thread for the fabric, stitch and garment being developed. Natural fibers have to be stitched with natural threads, for example, and man-made fabrics with man-made threads. The thread you select ought to have the identical attributes of your fabric, from compounds used to the fabric color. If not, the garment you have actually stitched is not going to be compatible with the laundering technique, resulting in your garment coming out un-repairable and disheveled.

In case you utilize a man-made thread with a natural fabric which shrinks when cleaned, the man-made thread is not going to shrink, leaving your thread loose. In case you utilize natural thread with a man-made fabric which doesn't shrink naturally, the natural thread is going to shrink throughout laundering, resulting in your garment being buckled. Understand the fabric compound you have actually bought and buy your thread appropriately. If you remain in doubt, request help.

Chapter 12-- Conclusion

The greatest pleasure in dressmaking is that you can produce your own design, who you see yourself as, through your own eyes. You can produce a custom within your own household, or you never know, you might simply create the next huge fashion break. There are no genuine guidelines regarding what one views as fashion, so the design realm is a blank canvas simply waiting for your contribution.

You may do this by producing the new great sundress or be Avant-Garde and blow everyone away at the red carpet event. You could revive something old and make it new once again or take elements from numerous periods and develop something totally new. You could follow a manufacturer's pattern, produce your own, or utilize old dresses as your influence. You could blend and match fabrics to produce flow or texture.

With really minimal sewing background, and with only a bit of practice, you could be developing your own dresses. This is your chance to add your own touches to your closet, include your own character, and utilize your imagination. Utilize this book as your guide, let your creative juices flow; the opportunities are limitless. Sewing dresses is enjoyable, lively, and worry-free! You can produce a romantic evening gown or a flirty and fun sports dress. You could stitch a range of dresses to fit any state of mind or event. Create your own style declaration. Soon, your closet is going to be overrun with dresses.

I hope that you enjoyed reading through this book and that you have found it useful. If you want to share your thoughts on this book, you can do so by leaving a review on the Amazon page. Have a great rest of the day.